EMPLOYEE MORALE AND PRODUCTIV ITY

THE SIMPLE MODERN GUIDES & SECRETS, SUCCESSFUL PEOPLE UNDERSTAND TIME MANAGEMENT AND HOW TO BALANCE WORK AND FESTIVITIES (BILLIONAIRES' HABITS)

RICHARD N. WILLIAMS

TABLE OF CONTENTS

INTRODUCTI ON

In the clamoring city of Progress View, where cutoff times and requests frequently eclipsed the delight of day to day existence, there stood an uninspiring place of business - the base camp of Zenith Developments. The air inside those walls was thick with the murmur of efficiency, however it missed the mark on amiability of the human soul.

In the midst of the ocean of work areas and vast columns of PC screens, there was a momentous individual named Sander Turner. Sander , a venture supervisor known for her resolute commitment, ended up remaining at the intersection of adjusting worker resolve and efficiency during the happy season.

The story starts not with a hackneyed "sometime in the distant past," however with Sander 's acknowledgment that the energy of the Christmas season could be saddled to motivate development and lift worker spirit. She considered how to imbue the soul of merriment without compromising the tenacious quest for greatness that characterized Peak Developments.

Sander 's most memorable move was inconspicuous yet significant. With tasteful decorations that made the office feel warm and inviting, she changed the environment. The standard sterile desk areas became merry safe houses, enhanced with glimmering lights and beautiful decorations. A common tree stood tall in the middle, and every division contributed special high quality enrichments, cultivating a feeling of solidarity and imagination.

Sander came up with themed "Innovation Breaks," which were short, structured intervals during which employees could participate in collaborative, non-work-related activities. She was aware that balance was necessary. These breaks became impetuses for cross-departmental holding, igniting discussions that rose above project timetables and notices.

The outcome was an organization of interconnected personalities, each contributing a remarkable viewpoint to the organization's aggregate insight.

Sander planned a series of celebration-themed team-building activities as the holiday season progressed. From gingerbread house rivalries to Secret St Nick trades, representatives got themselves teaming up on projects as well as sharing snapshots of euphoria outside the unbending bounds of their sets of responsibilities. The giggling reverberating through the lobbies turned into a demonstration of the revived soul inside the labor force.

Notwithstanding, the genuine defining moment came when Sander started a novel program called "Appreciation Narratives." Employees were encouraged to highlight the characteristics that made them exceptional team members and to express gratitude for their coworkers through a digital platform that was shared. Positivo energy flourished in The Chronicles, where previously unseen efforts of individuals became visible threads in a tapestry of appreciation.

Sander 's groundbreaking methodology started yielding unmistakable outcomes. Efficiency levels stayed high, and representatives detailed a recently discovered feeling of direction and kinship. The workplace, when described by the dullness of schedule, presently beats with the heartbeat of aggregate energy.

As the year attracted nearby, Peak Developments found itself meeting as well as unparalleled its objectives. The company's success was due in large part to the tenacity that Sander had fostered. The inclusion of festivities had not hindered productivity, which was a surprising development; It was now serving as the impetus for a cultural shift that placed an emphasis on both personal well-being and collaborative excellence.

The peak of this extraordinary excursion came during the organization's year-end festivity. Rather than a conventional office party, Sander coordinated an intelligent social occasion where workers shared individual and expert features of the year. A palpable sense of accomplishment that transcended any numerical target was felt, as were tears of gratitude and laughter brought on by shared memories.

Eventually, Sander Turner's imaginative way to deal with adjusting work and celebrations had raised representative resolve as well as established the groundwork for a work environment culture that esteemed the human soul as much as the quest for greatness. As the clock struck 12 PM on New Year's Eve, the representatives of Peak Developments embraced the future with a recharged feeling of direction and a common obligation to proceed with their excursion of advancement, flexibility, and aggregate achievement.

Definition of Employee Morale

Representative spirit alludes to the general fulfillment, mentality, and excitement that representatives feel toward their work and the association they are a piece of. It has a significant impact on productivity, job satisfaction, and ultimately a company's success in the workplace. The meaning of representative assurance goes past simple joy; it envelops the close to home prosperity, inspiration, and feeling of having a place that people insight in their expert jobs.

Morale among employees is fundamentally a reflection of a workforce's collective mood and mindset. Workplace culture, leadership style, interpersonal relationships, compensation, recognition, and opportunities for professional growth all have an impact on this dynamic and multifaceted concept. High confidence is described by uplifting perspectives, a solid hard working attitude, and a readiness to exceed everyone's expectations in adding to the association's objectives.

One vital component of worker spirit is work fulfillment. At the point when workers find satisfaction and reason in their jobs, it straightforwardly affects their general confidence. Work fulfillment is frequently attached to elements like significant work, a feeling of achievement, and the acknowledgment of one's commitments. On the other hand, low levels of job satisfaction can lower morale, which in turn can increase absenteeism, employee turnover, and lower performance.

Successful authority assumes a significant part in forming and keeping up with high worker spirit. Employees feel valued and understood in the workplace when leaders are open, communicative, and supportive. Trust is a foundation of positive resolve; at the point when workers trust their chiefs, they are bound to be locked in and propelled. On the other hand, a lack of communication, inconsistent decision-making, or lack of empathy in leadership can lower morale and create a hostile work environment.

Acknowledgment and appreciation are strong drivers of worker resolve. At the point when people feel recognized for their endeavors and achievements, it encourages a good climate. Acknowledgment can take different structures, including verbal applause, grants, or even basic articulations of appreciation. An absence of acknowledgment, then again, can prompt sensations of unappreciation and add to a decrease in spirit.

Employee morale is also significantly impacted by interpersonal relationships and a sense of community among coworkers in the workplace. Positive connections, coordinated effort, and a strong group climate add to a feeling of having a place and local area. On the other hand, a poisonous or unfriendly work environment culture can negatively affect spirit, prompting pressure, tension, and an absence of inspiration.

Pay and advantages are extra factors that impact worker assurance. While cutthroat compensation and alluring advantages are not the sole determinants of spirit, they really do add to a singular's general fulfillment with their business. Fair pay mirrors an organization's obligation to perceiving and remunerating workers for their commitments, decidedly influencing confidence.

Potential open doors for proficient turn of events and professional success are pivotal for keeping up with high worker assurance. At the point when people see a make way for development inside an association, it improves their feeling of direction and responsibility. On the other hand, an absence of vocation improvement open doors might prompt stagnation and reduced confidence.

Morale among workers is not a fixed state; rather, it is a dynamic and changing aspect of the workplace. It requires continuous consideration and venture from initiative to establish and support a positive workplace. Customary correspondence, criticism systems, and endeavors to address concerns add to a culture that focuses on representative prosperity and spirit.

All in all, the meaning of worker resolve envelops the in general profound prosperity, fulfillment, and inspiration of pooplo incide a working environment. It is impacted by different variables, including administration, work fulfillment, acknowledgment, working environment culture, and open doors for development. High worker resolve is related with uplifting outlooks, expanded efficiency, and a feeling of direction among representatives. On the other hand, low spirit can prompt diminished work fulfillment, higher turnover, and an adverse consequence on hierarchical achievement. Perceiving the significance of representative spirit and effectively attempting to improve it is fundamental for cultivating a solid and flourishing work environment.

Importance of Employee Productivity

Productivity among workers is a crucial aspect of any business's success. It includes the productivity and adequacy with which workers add to the accomplishment of authoritative objectives. The significance of worker efficiency couldn't possibly be more significant, as it straightforwardly influences different parts of a business, from its primary concern to its general seriousness on the lookout.

One of the essential justifications for why representative efficiency is significant is its immediate relationship to authoritative execution. At the point when workers are useful, they offer more to the organization's result, bringing about expanded proficiency and viability. This, thus, can prompt higher benefits and a superior monetary situation for the association. Useful representatives are bound to comply with time constraints, convey quality work, and adjust to changing business needs, all of which add to generally achievement.

Also, representative efficiency is firmly connected to consumer loyalty. Delivering goods or services promptly and effectively is essential for maintaining a positive customer experience in today's competitive business environment. Useful workers guarantee that clients get what they need expeditiously, prompting expanded consumer loyalty and dependability. Customers who are satisfied are more likely to buy from the business again and to recommend it to others, which has a positive effect on the company's reputation and position in the market.

Productivity among employees also plays a crucial role in encouraging innovation within an organization. Employees have time and energy to think creatively and contribute new ideas when they are productive. This imaginative mentality can prompt the improvement of new items, administrations, or cycles, giving the organization an upper hand on the lookout. On the other hand, low productivity may stifle creativity and make it difficult for the business to adjust to changes or take advantage of new opportunities.

Besides, the significance of worker efficiency reaches out to representative commitment and occupation fulfillment. Drawn in and fulfilled representatives are bound to be useful and focused on their work. Creating a positive work environment, providing opportunities for professional development, and recognizing and rewarding employees for their contributions are all common investments made by businesses that place a high value on employee productivity. This lifts efficiency as well as assists in holding with garnish ability, decreasing turnover expenses, and cultivating a positive hierarchical culture.

Representative efficiency is likewise intently attached to cost administration. Wasteful work cycles, postponements, and errors can prompt expanded functional expenses for a business. On the other hand, an organization's resources can be maximized, waste can be reduced, and costs can be reduced when employees are productive. This cost reserve funds can be diverted towards vital drives, further adding to the organization's drawn out progress.

Monitoring and increasing employee productivity have become even more important in the age of remote and flexible work arrangements. Remote work offers adaptability yet additionally presents difficulties concerning correspondence, joint effort, and keeping a feeling of responsibility.

Associations need to carry out techniques and devices to quantify and further develop efficiency in a virtual workplace. This might incorporate embracing joint effort stages, giving preparation on using time effectively, and cultivating a culture of trust and open correspondence.

Perceiving the significance of representative efficiency, numerous associations put resources into innovation and instruments to smooth out work processes. Digital solutions, such as project management software and automation, can aid in the reduction of manual errors, the elimination of repetitive tasks, and overall efficiency. By utilizing innovation, organizations can engage their representatives to zero in on undertakings that require imagination, decisive reasoning, and critical thinking, prompting a more useful and satisfying work insight.

All in all, the significance of representative efficiency couldn't possibly be more significant in that frame of mind of any association. It influences hierarchical execution, consumer loyalty, advancement, worker commitment, cost administration, and flexibility to evolving conditions. It is essential for long-term sustainability and competitiveness for businesses to prioritize and invest in strategies to increase employee productivity as they navigate an evolving landscape.

Overview of Balancing Work and Festivities

Adjusting work and merriments is a many-sided dance that people perform, endeavoring to keep up with proficient responsibilities while enjoying the glad soul of festivities. The challenge gets harder to deal with as the holiday season gets closer, necessitating strategic thinking and careful planning to find the right balance.

This delicate balancing act essentially entails effective time management. Workers frequently wind up conflicted between fulfilling project time constraints and taking part in merry occasions. The vitality lies in laying out needs and making a reasonable timetable that obliges both work and festivities. This necessitates a proactive attitude in which individuals anticipate and plan for their holiday workloads.

In the workplace, effective communication is critical. Understanding and collaboration are cultivated when coworkers and supervisors are made aware of the potential difficulties in meeting deadlines brought on by holiday obligations. Communication that is open and honest makes it easier to set realistic expectations and fosters a supportive workplace where coworkers can work together to get through the hustle and bustle of the holidays.

Innovation ends up being an important partner in this undertaking. The ascent of remote work and computerized specialized devices empowers people to satisfy proficient obligations while not truly present at the workplace. Employees are empowered to participate in celebrations without compromising productivity thanks to this flexibility, which facilitates a smoother integration of work and festivities.

Moreover, during the holiday season, employers are crucial in promoting a healthy work-life balance. Offering adaptable work hours, conceding extra downtime, or coordinating vast festivals can add to a positive workplace. Employee loyalty is cultivated and overall job satisfaction is raised when employers acknowledge the significance of both personal and professional aspects in employees' lives.

Notwithstanding, the test reaches out past using time productively and into the mental domain. Adjusting work and merriments requires a careful change between work mode and celebratory mode. Whether you're tackling a project deadline or enjoying a festive gathering, compartmentalizing tasks and being present in the moment are key. Individuals can fully engage in both spheres without feeling overwhelmed by the ability to mentally switch gears.

Critically, taking care of oneself becomes non-debatable during this period. The strain to meet work responsibilities while effectively taking part in celebrations can prompt burnout assuming that people disregard their prosperity. It is essential to successfully navigate this delicate balance by prioritizing adequate rest, maintaining a healthy lifestyle, and incorporating moments of relaxation amid the chaos of the holidays.

The dynamics of balancing work and celebrations reflect the changing nature of work culture in a broader societal context. A more adaptable and holistic approach is required as the traditional boundaries between personal and professional life are becoming increasingly fuzzier. Associations that perceive and embrace this shift are better situated to draw in and hold ability in a cutthroat scene.

As working environments become more different, recognizing and regarding different social and strict festivals is indispensable to encouraging inclusivity. Associations can assume a part in establishing a climate where people from various foundations feel esteemed and upheld during their separate merry seasons. This inclusivity upgrades group union and adds to a positive hierarchical culture.

The overview of how to strike a balance between work and fun demonstrates the complexity of modern life, in which people strive to excel in their professional roles while cherishing the joyful celebrations. Fruitful route of this fragile equilibrium includes successful using time effectively, straightforward correspondence, innovative incorporation, mental nimbleness, and a pledge to taking care of oneself. For fostering a healthy and productive workforce, adopting a holistic approach that acknowledges the significance of both personal and professional aspects is essential as work culture continues to change.

Chapter 1
The Impact of Festivities on Employee Morale

Celebrations assume a pivotal part in molding the working environment climate and can fundamentally affect representative resolve. These celebratory occasions, going from occasion gatherings to group building exercises, add to a positive and dynamic air inside the association. Understanding the elements of this effect is fundamental for businesses trying to cultivate a persuasion and connection with the labor force.

Fostering a sense of community and camaraderie is one of the primary ways that celebrations boost employee morale. Celebrating extraordinary events together permits partners to interface on an individual level, past their expert jobs. Shared encounters during merry occasions make securities among colleagues, separating correspondence boundaries and advancing a more strong workplace. This feeling of having a place is a strong inspiration, as representatives feel esteemed for their work commitments as well as people with remarkable interests and characters.

Besides, celebrations give a much needed reprieve from the standard requests of the working environment. Whether it's a themed office party, a group building retreat, or a straightforward lunch assembly, these occasions offer workers a valuable chance to unwind and loosen up. Enjoying some time off from the monotonous routine permits people to re-energize their psychological and close to home batteries, diminishing pressure and forestalling burnout. The subsequent lift in feeling of confidence can prompt expanded efficiency and imagination, as workers return to their undertakings with reestablished energy and excitement.

Acknowledgment is one more pivotal part of the effect of celebrations on worker spirit. During festivities, managers frequently make a move to recognize and value the difficult work and commitment of their staff. Recognizing employees' contributions fosters a positive work environment and increases their sense of accomplishment, whether through symbolic gestures, personalized messages, or awards. Feeling appreciated and esteemed encourages areas of strength for an occupation fulfillment and faithfulness among colleagues.

By reaffirming shared values and objectives, festivities also contribute to a positive organizational culture. Praising accomplishments, achievements, and social or strict occasions helps fabricate a feeling of character inside the working environment. This common personality makes a more strong and brought together group, adjusting representatives to the organization's central goal and values. A solid hierarchical culture adds to a good workplace where people are bound to feel propelled and locked in.

Notwithstanding, it is fundamental for bosses to move toward celebrations with aversion to variety and consideration. Not all representatives praise similar occasions or offer similar social practices. Comprehensive festivals that perceive and regard different foundations add to a more strong and amicable working environment. Every employee should feel at ease participating in celebrations without having to compromise their own personal beliefs or values, so employers should strive to foster an inclusive work environment.

On the other hand, the nonappearance or misusing of bubbly festivals can have adverse results on representative spirit. An absence of acknowledgment for unique events or an inability to give valuable chances to mingling can prompt sensations of disregard and separation. Representatives might see the work environment as generic or unconcerned with their prosperity, bringing about a decrease in confidence and generally speaking position fulfillment.

celebrations have a variety of positive effects on the workplace and on employee morale. From encouraging a feeling of local area and brotherhood to giving a break from routine and perceiving worker commitments, festivities add to a good hierarchical culture. Be that as it may, it is vital for managers to move toward celebrations considering inclusivity, regarding the variety of their labor force. Eventually, a working environment that hugs and values celebrations is bound to have a propelled, drew in, and fulfilled labor force.

Positive Effects and Potential Challenges

The way we live, work, and communicate has been transformed by technological advancements, which have made them an integral part of our day-to-day lives. These developments achieve beneficial outcomes across different parts of society, yet they likewise present difficulties that require conscious thought. This paper investigates the beneficial outcomes and potential difficulties related with the steady walk of innovation.

Positive outcomes:

Further developed Correspondence:

Innovation has altered correspondence, making it quicker, more effective, and open all around the world. Web-based entertainment stages, informing applications, and video conferencing devices have crossed over holes and associated individuals in manners unbelievable only years and years prior.

Improved Schooling:

Innovation has reshaped the instruction scene, furnishing understudies with admittance to huge measures of data. Online courses, intelligent learning stages, and instructive applications work with customized opportunities for growth, taking special care of different necessities and learning styles.

Headways in Medical services:

Mechanical advancements have altogether further developed medical services results. Technology has improved the accuracy of medical diagnoses, streamlined patient care, and made it possible for remote consultations—especially important in times of global crises—through sophisticated diagnostic tools and telemedicine solutions.

Expanded Productivity in Work environments:

Robotization and computerized apparatuses have improved efficiency in working environments. Errands that once called for huge investment and labor supply can now be productively taken care of by machines, opening up HR to zero in on additional imaginative and complex parts of their positions.

Worldwide Availability:

The web has transformed the world into a worldwide town, cultivating network and cooperation on an exceptional scale. Organizations can work universally, specialists can team up across boundaries, and people can participate in multifaceted trades easily.

Natural Effect Alleviation:

Innovation can possibly address ecological difficulties. Developments, for example, environmentally friendly power sources, savvy frameworks, and energy-productive innovations add to the alleviation of environmental change and the advancement of supportable practices.

Possible Difficulties:

Work Relocation:

Concerns about widespread job displacement arise as a result of the threat posed by artificial intelligence and automation to particular job sectors As machines assume control over routine undertakings, there is a requirement for retraining and upskilling the labor force to adjust to the developing position market.

Privacy issues:

The rising dependence on innovation raises serious security concerns. The balance between innovation and the protection of individual privacy rights has been the subject of debate due to data breaches, surveillance, and tech companies' collection of personal information.

Computerized Gap:

Notwithstanding worldwide network, a computerized partition actually exists, with variations in admittance to innovation among princely and underestimated networks. This hole fuels existing disparities, upsetting open doors for instruction, work, and social investment.

Online protection Dangers:

The interconnected idea of innovation uncovered people and associations to network safety dangers. Malware, hacking, and other digital assaults can think twice about information, prompting monetary misfortunes and possible disturbances in basic foundation.

Social Seclusion:

The commonness of computerized correspondence has prompted worries about friendly disengagement. An excessive reliance on online interactions may reduce in-person connections, which may have an effect on mental health and social well-being.

Moral Predicaments:

Ethical guidelines are often developed at a slower rate than technological advancements. Regulation and careful consideration are required for issues like the ethical use of artificial intelligence, genetic engineering, and the impact of automation on societal values.

Although advancements in technology have many advantages, they also come with a number of disadvantages that necessitate thoughtful and proactive solutions. Finding some kind of harmony between embracing development and tending to potential downsides is critical for guaranteeing that innovation contributes emphatically to the general prosperity of people and society overall.

Consistent discourse, moral contemplations, and administrative structures are fundamental parts of exploring the perplexing scene of innovative advancement.

Chapter 2 Strategies for Maintaining Morale During Festive Periods

Keeping up with high resolve during merry periods is pivotal for cultivating a positive workplace and guaranteeing efficiency. The Christmas season, set apart by festivities and downtime, can in some cases lead to a dunk in inspiration and concentration among workers. Managers and pioneers should carry out viable procedures to neutralize this likely decrease in assurance. The following are a few vital ways to deal with keep spirits high during bubbly periods.

1. Adaptable Booking:
Taking into account adaptable plans for getting work done during the happy season can assist representatives with adjusting their expert and individual responsibilities. Whether it's changing working hours or carrying out remote work choices, this adaptability can add to a more loosened up environment,

decreasing pressure and expanding generally work fulfillment.

2. Acknowledgment and Prizes:

Recognizing representatives' diligent effort and devotion during the merry season is fundamental. Carrying out an acknowledgment and prizes program can lift the general mood by causing people to feel esteemed. This can be expressed verbally, in personalized notes, or even in the form of tangible rewards like gift cards or bonuses. Perceiving accomplishments and achievements can make a positive climate inside the working environment.

3. Bubbly Adornments and Exercises:

Changing the work environment into a bubbly and blissful space can fundamentally influence representatives' temperament and inspiration. A sense of community and shared celebration can be created by decorating the office, organizing themed events, or encouraging team-building activities related to the holiday season. This encourages a positive climate that stretches out past the workplace errands.

4. Clear Correspondence:

Successful correspondence is pivotal in keeping up with assurance. Manage uncertainty and stress by providing clear information about holiday schedules, expectations, and any changes to work routines. Staying with workers informed about plans and drives during the bubbly time frame keeps a feeling of straightforwardness and trust.

5. Downtime and Rest:

While it might appear to be nonsensical, empowering workers to get some much needed rest during the bubbly season is fundamental. This permits them to re-energize and invest quality energy with loved ones. Bosses ought to effectively advance a sound balance between serious and fun activities and put exorbitant work during occasions down. This approach adds to long haul work fulfillment and representative prosperity.

6. Initiatives for Employee Engagement:

Connecting with representatives in dynamic cycles and looking for their contribution on bubbly exercises or occasions can upgrade their feeling of having a place. This collaborative approach empowers individuals to actively contribute to the creation of a festive atmosphere and fosters a positive work environment.

7. Assistance with Personal Growth:

By showing employees that their development is a priority, providing opportunities for personal and professional growth, such as workshops or training sessions, can boost morale. Putting resources into their abilities and information helps the person as well as adds to the general outcome of the organization.

8. Chipping in and Corporate Social Obligation:

Empowering representatives to take part in volunteer exercises or add to worthy missions during the merry season can give a feeling of motivation and satisfaction. Corporate social obligation drives benefit the local area as well as make a positive picture of the organization, lifting worker pride and feeling of confidence.

9. Group building Activities:

Organizing team-building activities or retreats during the holiday season can improve coworker relationships. This can improve joint effort, correspondence, and collaboration, prompting a more firm and inspired labor force.

10. Appreciation and Positive Criticism:

Gratitude and constructive criticism are easy but effective ways to boost morale. Pioneers ought to consistently recognize and value the endeavors of their colleagues, encouraging a culture of energy and shared help.

All in all, keeping up with high spirit during happy periods requires a blend of adaptability, acknowledgment, correspondence, and commitment drives. By establishing a steady and positive workplace, managers can guarantee that representatives stay roused and fulfilled, adding to both individual achievement and the general outcome of the association.

Flexible Work Schedules and Team-Building Activities

Adaptable plans for getting work done and group building exercises are indispensable parts of present day work environment methodologies, cultivating a dynamic and agreeable climate. Approaches to employee engagement and productivity change over time within an organization. This shift is obvious in the rising commonness of adaptable plans for getting work done and the accentuation in group building exercises, both contributing essentially to a positive work culture.

Adaptable plans for getting work done affect representative prosperity and execution. The customary all day average business day is steadily being supplanted by additional versatile courses of action, for example, strategic scheduling, compacted work filled weeks, and remote work choices. This shift recognizes the different necessities of a labor force containing people with fluctuating ways of life and obligations.

One vital benefit of adaptable plans for getting work done is further developed balance between serious and fun activities. Representatives can tailor their work hours to oblige individual responsibilities, prompting diminished pressure and burnout. At the point when representatives have the adaptability to adjust work and life actually, they are bound to stay drew in and roused. This, thus, adds to higher work fulfillment and consistency standards.

Moreover, adaptable plans for getting work done can improve efficiency by permitting representatives to work during their most useful hours. Not every person works ideally inside the bounds of a conventional all day plan. By enabling representatives to pick when they work, associations tap into individual efficiency tops, bringing about more productive and centered work.

Remote work, a conspicuous part of adaptable timetables, has become progressively common, especially following worldwide occasions that have sped up the reception of virtual joint effort devices. Remote work not just gives representatives the opportunity to pick their workplace yet in addition extends the ability pool for associations. Managers can get to a different cluster of abilities and viewpoints from anyplace on the planet, encouraging development and innovativeness inside the group.

In any case, the shift to adaptable plans for getting work done likewise presents difficulties, for example, the potential for correspondence holes and sensations of separation among telecommuters. To alleviate these issues, associations should put resources into strong specialized instruments and lay out clear rules for distant joint effort. Normal virtual gatherings, group registrations, and cooperative stages assist with keeping a feeling of association among colleagues, no matter what their actual areas.

Supplementing adaptable plans for getting work done, group building exercises assume a pivotal part in areas of strength for encouraging connections and a positive hierarchical culture. These exercises go past conventional icebreakers and trust falls, incorporating a scope of encounters intended to reinforce cooperation, correspondence, and fellowship among colleagues.

Activities for building teams can take many different forms, from retreats and workshops in the outdoors to virtual games and challenges. No matter what the organization, the objective is to set out open doors for workers to interface on an individual level, separating obstructions and building trust. This sense of community extends to the workplace, resulting in enhanced teamwork and collaboration.

Besides, group building exercises add to a positive workplace by infusing a component of fun into the expert circle. At the point when workers partake in their time together and share positive encounters, it makes a feeling of having a place and supports an aggregate personality inside the group. This, thus, affects confidence, inspiration, and generally speaking position fulfillment.

For remote groups, virtual group building exercises have turned into a pivotal instrument for cultivating association and commitment. These exercises influence video conferencing stages and online joint effort instruments to make shared encounters regardless of actual distances. Online games, interactive workshops, and virtual escape rooms help remote teams develop relationships, communicate effectively, and overcome the difficulties of working from different locations.

Be that as it may, the outcome of group building exercises depends on smart preparation and arrangement with the group's elements. Pioneers should consider the inclinations and solace levels of colleagues, guaranteeing that exercises are comprehensive and pleasant for everybody. By fitting group building drives to the exceptional qualities of the group, pioneers can fortify bonds and make a positive group culture.

All in all, adaptable plans for getting work done and group building exercises are crucial components of a cutting edge working environment endeavoring to upgrade representative fulfillment, efficiency, and generally speaking prosperity. The shift towards adaptability perceives the distinction of representatives, advancing balance between fun and serious activities and obliging different ways of life. At the same time, group building exercises cultivate a feeling of local area and coordinated effort, whether face to face or essentially, adding to a good and firm hierarchical culture. Organizations can adapt to the changing needs of their workforce by incorporating these practices and cultivating work environments where employees thrive personally and professionally.

Recognition and Rewards

Organizational culture and performance are profoundly influenced by rewards and recognition. Whether in a corporate setting, instructive establishment, or local gathering, recognizing and valuing people for their commitments cultivates a positive climate and propels them with greatness.

Recognizing one's efforts and achievements is an effective strategy. It goes past simple affirmation, diving into the mental domain where people feel esteemed and appreciated. This affirmation can take different structures, from a basic "much obliged" to more formalized acknowledgment programs.

Employee engagement and contentment tend to rise in the workplace when recognition is given. Employees are more likely to be motivated and committed to their work when they perceive that their efforts are recognized and appreciated. This encouraging feedback can add to a better work culture, cultivating coordinated effort and a feeling of having a place.

Besides, acknowledgment fills in as an impetus for nonstop improvement. At the point when people realize their endeavors are remembered, they are urged to take a stab at greatness and contribute their best to the group. This positive pattern of affirmation and improvement establishes a unique workplace where representatives are propelled to develop and upgrade their abilities.

Interestingly, an absence of acknowledgment can prompt demotivation and separation. Representatives who feel their persistent effort slips through the cracks might become frustrated, influencing their efficiency and by and large work fulfillment. This can eventually bring about high turnover rates, as people look for conditions where their commitments are cotoomod.

Rewarding someone adds a tangible element to the appreciation process while recognition provides the emotional aspect of acknowledgment. Prizes can go from money related motivators and rewards to non-financial advantages like adaptable work hours, proficient advancement, open doors, or even open acknowledgment functions.

Money related rewards, for example, rewards or execution based pay, are in many cases compelling in rousing workers to accomplish explicit targets. Be that as it may, it's essential to offset these with non-money related prizes to take care of a different scope of representative inclinations.

In addition to contributing to a positive work environment, non-monetary incentives demonstrate a commitment to the well-being of employees beyond financial considerations.

In instructive settings, acknowledgment and prizes are similarly crucial. Understudies flourish when their endeavors are recognized, whether through acclaim from educators, authentications of accomplishment, or different types of affirmation. In education, positive reinforcement not only helps people feel more confident, but it also helps them develop a love of learning and a sense of accomplishment.

Acknowledgement and prizes are likewise instrumental in building serious areas of strength for any local area. In volunteer associations or local gatherings, people commit their time and exertion without monetary pay.

Recognizing their commitments through open acknowledgment, appreciation occasions, or declarations of appreciation becomes vital in supporting their responsibility and excitement.

To carry out compelling acknowledgment and prizes programs, associations should fit their ways to deal with the exceptional requirements and inclinations of their individuals. Understanding individual inspirations, whether characteristic or outward, assists in planning programs that reverberate with different crowds.

Standard criticism components can support refining these projects, guaranteeing they stay applicable and effective after some time.

All in all, acknowledgement and prizes are basic parts of encouraging a positive and useful climate in different settings. Whether in the work environment, instructive foundations, or local gatherings, recognizing people for their commitments lifts the general mood as well as drives nonstop improvement and responsibility.

Adjusting both close to home acknowledgment and unmistakable prizes makes an all encompassing way to deal with appreciation, adding to the general achievement and prosperity of people and the associations they serve.

Chapter 3 Successful Examples of Balancing Work and Festivities

Adjusting work and merriments can be a difficult accomplishment, yet there are a few fruitful models that exhibit how people and associations have successfully figured out how to combine proficient obligations with the euphoric soul of festivities. These models show the significance of making an amicable balance between fun and serious activities during happy seasons.

Google's approach to maintaining a festive atmosphere in its workplace is a notable example. Google's reputation for encouraging creative and upbeat work environments extends to its holiday celebrations. The organization frequently enriches its workplaces with bubbly subjects, sorts out group building exercises, and urges representatives to partake in occasion related occasions. By coordinating festivals into the work schedule, Google lifts representative feeling of confidence as well as develops a feeling of local area.

Also, a few organizations carry out adaptable work hours during bubbly seasons, perceiving the requirement for representatives to oversee individual and family responsibilities. For example, Salesforce, a worldwide distributed computing organization, has been known to embrace an adaptable work strategy during significant occasions. This permits representatives to tweak their work hours, working with a more adjusted way to deal with expert and individual obligations.

In the domain of business venture, private companies like neighborhood pastry kitchens or gift shops frequently track down imaginative ways of mixing work and merriments. These organizations might send off unique occasion themed items or administrations, making a celebratory air for the two representatives and clients. By adjusting their contributions to the happy soul, these organizations improve client commitment as well as inject a feeling of satisfaction into the work environment.

On a singular level, experts can take on procedures to actually deal with their work responsibilities while getting a charge out of celebrations. Using time effectively becomes vital during such periods. Setting clear priorities and deadlines, which allow people to concentrate on important tasks without feeling overwhelmed by the hustle and bustle of the holidays, is one successful practice. This approach keeps up with efficiency while leaving space for individual festivals.

Another powerful procedure includes utilizing innovation to smooth out work processes. With the approach of remote work instruments and correspondence stages, people can team up consistently from various areas. Professionals can take part in virtual celebrations or spend quality time with loved ones while still meeting their work obligations. Video conferencing, project the executives applications, and other computerized devices add to a more adaptable and versatile workplace.

Additionally, boundary-setting is emphasized by some successful professionals during festive seasons. By obviously characterizing when work starts and closures, people can distribute explicit time allotments for both expert and individual exercises. This proactive methodology limits the gamble of work infringing on happy minutes as well as the other way around, cultivating a better balance between serious and fun activities.

In the domain of public help, legislatures and public foundations likewise assume a part in establishing a favorable climate for work and merriments. Government offices in some nations may operate with fewer employees or offer fewer services during official holiday periods. This recognizes the meaning of merriments as well as permits community workers to take part in festivals without undermining their expert responsibilities.

Additionally, effective instances of adjusting work and celebrations can be tracked down in the domain of occasion the board. Large-scale events like festivals and celebrations are often organized and carried out by professionals in this field who frequently put in long hours. In spite of the requesting idea of their work, occasion organizers epitomize powerful using time effectively and fastidious wanting to guarantee the progress of both business related projects and the bubbly events they work with.

there are numerous successful examples of balancing work and celebrations. Whether it's through broad drives, adaptable work arrangements, imaginative business procedures, individual time usage practices, or government-drove draws near, the vital lies in perceiving the significance of fitting proficient obligations with the delight of festivities. These models act as motivation for people and associations looking to establish a workplace that embraces the soul of celebrations while keeping an elevated degree of efficiency and fulfillment.

Chapter 4
Challenges in Balancing Work and Festivities

Adjusting work and merriments represents a heap of difficulties that people wrestle with, particularly in a quick moving and requesting world. The conflict between professional responsibilities and the desire to participate in festive celebrations becomes palpable as the holiday season approaches. The battle to keep up with balance in these clashing spaces isn't just an individual test yet additionally a cultural one that mirrors the developing idea of work-life elements.

One critical test is the strain to comply with work time constraints in the midst of the cheerful air of celebrations. As organizations endeavor to keep up with efficiency, representatives frequently wind up exploring weighty jobs during when their psyches might be leaned towards occasion cheer. The battle to zero in on assignments while dreams of occasion beautifications dance in one's mind can prompt elevated feelings of anxiety and diminished work fulfillment.

Besides, the advanced age has obscured the limits among expert and individual life. The blurring of the lines between personal time and office hours is made more difficult by the constant connectivity provided by smartphones and remote work arrangements. During merry seasons, the assumption to stay receptive to work messages and messages can encroach upon valuable minutes implied for praising with loved ones.

An additional significant aspect of celebrations, family obligations, adds complexity. The longing to invest quality energy with friends and family conflicts with work responsibilities, prompting a fragile difficult exercise. Feelings of inadequacy and stress can be exacerbated by guilt over missing family gatherings or not being fully present because of work obligations.

Besides, the monetary strain related with the Christmas season intensifies the difficulties of balance between serious and fun activities. People might feel a sense of urgency to take on extra work or extra time to manage the cost of gifts, travel, and other happy costs. This quest for monetary solidness can result in burnout, as the requests of work heighten exactly when individual time is desired the most.

The strain to adjust to cultural assumptions and keep a veneer of seasonal happiness can likewise strain people. The apprehension about judgment or expert repercussions might lead people to focus on work over celebrations, forfeiting their own delight for apparent expert commitment. The difficulties of balancing work and celebrations in a harmonious manner are exacerbated by this internal conflict between personal desires and societal expectations.

During festive seasons, employers also play a crucial role in shaping the work environment. A toxic work environment can be caused by a lack of clear policies or resources for employees struggling with work-life balance. Alternately, organizations that perceive the significance of representative prosperity during bubbly periods might carry out adaptable timetables, remote work choices, or extra downtime to ease the weight on their labor force.

Effective time management and prioritization are required to maintain a work-life balance. Preparing, setting sensible assumptions, and discussing straightforwardly with partners and managers can assist with moderating the pressure related with shuffling proficient and individual responsibilities. Making limits, both physical and advanced, is essential to defending devoted time for merry exercises without settling on work liabilities.

Taking a proactive approach to work-life balance necessitates acknowledging the imminence of obstacles and devising solutions to them. This might incorporate assigning undertakings, laying out sensible objectives, and figuring out how to say no when fundamental. Businesses can add to a better workplace by cultivating a culture that values prosperity, energizes open correspondence, and offers the essential help structures.

All in all, the difficulties in adjusting work and merriments are diverse, originating from cultural assumptions, individual yearnings, and the advancing idea of work. Exploring this fragile harmony requires a blend of mindfulness, compelling correspondence, and a strong workplace. A nuanced and adaptable approach is essential for fostering a harmonious and fulfilling balance between the professional and personal spheres as individuals and organizations strive to reconcile the demands of work with the joys of festive celebrations.

Workload Management and Maintaining Focus

To achieve productivity and avoid burnout, effective workload management and maintaining focus are essential. People frequently find themselves juggling multiple tasks simultaneously in our fast-paced and demanding work environments. Effectively exploring this scene requires an essential way to deal with responsibility, the board and a pledge to support concentration in the midst of interruptions.

Responsibility the board includes improving the dissemination of errands, guaranteeing that cutoff times are met, and forestalling a mind-boggling amassing of liabilities. One key angle is prioritization. Not all undertakings are made equivalent, and recognizing dire and significant tasks is essential. The Eisenhower Lattice, a well known efficiency device, sorts undertakings into four quadrants in view of earnestness and significance. This model urges people to zero in on undertakings that line up with long haul objectives and contribute altogether to generally speaking achievement.

Moreover, compelling responsibility the board includes defining reasonable objectives and cutoff times. Unreasonable assumptions can prompt pressure and diminished execution. It's fundamental to survey the time expected for each undertaking everything being equal and distribute assets appropriately. Utilizing time-usage methods like the Pomodoro Strategy, where work is broken into spans with brief intervals in the middle between, can improve concentration and efficiency.

Appointing errands is one more key part of the responsibility of the board. Perceiving when to appoint permits people to focus on high-need exercises that require their extraordinary abilities. In addition to distributing the work, delegation encourages teamwork and skill development within an organization or team.

Notwithstanding the task of the executives, keeping up with the center is similarly crucial for supported efficiency. The advanced workplace is overflowing with interruptions, from consistent warnings to the bait of online entertainment. It is essential to Execute systems to limit interferences. This might include switching off insignificant notices, making assigned periods for centered work, or using apparatuses that block diverting sites during work hours.

Care practices can altogether add to keeping up with the center. Methods, for example, contemplation and profound breathing activities assist people with developing the capacity to divert their thoughtfulness regarding the job needing to be done. Care improves focus as well as adds to general prosperity, decreasing pressure and expanding flexibility.

It is important to create a working environment that is conducive to concentration. A messiness free and coordinated work area can limit visual interruptions and make a helpful air for centered work. Besides, ergonomic contemplations, for example, happy with seating and legitimate lighting, assume a part in improving focus and forestalling actual distress that could prompt interruption.

Defining limits is a basic part of keeping up with the center. Obviously characterized work hours and breaks assist people with dealing with their energy levels really. Workaholic behavior can prompt burnout and a decrease in efficiency. Laying out a harmony among work and individual life is fundamental for long haul achievement and prosperity.

Standard breaks are fundamental for keeping up with center as well as add to by and large efficiency. The human cerebrum works ideally with intermittent rest, and brief breaks can forestall mental weariness. Going for a walk, participating in a concise work-out everyday practice, or essentially moving back from the workplace during breaks can recharge people and improve their capacity to think when they return to their undertakings.

Viable correspondence is another element that impacts responsibility, the executives and concentration. Clear correspondence inside a group guarantees that everybody is in total agreement in regards to objectives, cutoff times, and assumptions. Miscommunication can prompt disarray, pointless pressure, and diminished center around fundamental undertakings. Standard group gatherings, updates, and input meetings work with a cooperative and very much educated workplace.

Consistent mastering and expertise advancement are vital to remaining on track and versatile in the present powerful work scene. Embracing new advances, remaining refreshed on industry patterns, and procuring extra abilities improve a singular's worth as well as add to a development outlook that encourages flexibility and concentration notwithstanding challenges.

All in all, compelling responsibility for the executives and keeping up with the center are interconnected parts of accomplishing efficiency and prosperity in the working environment. Prioritization, reasonable objective setting, designation, care rehearses, and a favorable workplace add to proficient responsibility the board. Maintaining focus simultaneously necessitates fostering effective communication, setting boundaries, taking regular breaks, and minimizing distractions. Individuals can successfully navigate the demands of their roles, prevent burnout, and foster a career that is both fulfilling and sustainable by incorporating these strategies into their daily work routines.

Chapter 5
Measuring Employee Morale and Productivity

Organizations that want to create a positive work environment and achieve optimal performance must measure employee morale and productivity. Understanding the variables that impact these angles permits organizations to carry out designated procedures for development. This extensive examination investigates different strategies and key markers in checking both representative confidence and efficiency.

Worker Assurance Estimation:

Reviews and Input:

Leading customary reviews is a basic way to deal with measure representative spirit. Specific topics like job satisfaction, work-life balance, and teamwork can be addressed by custom questionnaires. Unknown input supports legit reactions, giving important bits of knowledge into the labor force's opinions.

One-on-One Meetings:

Individual meetings with workers consider a more inside and out investigation of individual encounters and concerns. This subjective methodology reveals nuanced feelings and discernments that probably won't surface in overviews. It likewise exhibits a guarantee to understanding and tending to individual necessities.

Worker Help Projects (EAPs):

Not only does the use of EAPs help employees who are going through personal difficulties, but it also indirectly shows how morale is doing. The recurrence of EAP use can mirror the degree of stress or disappointment inside the labor force.

Participation and Dependability:

Reliable participation and reliability are characteristic of a positive workplace. An expansion in non-attendance or successive lateness might flag basic confidence issues. Observing these examples can be a direct measurement for checking generally worker fulfillment.

Worker Turnover Rates:

High turnover rates frequently relate with low resolve. At the point when representatives are disappointed, they are bound to look for elective business. It's helpful to keep tabs on turnover rates over time to get a sense of how well the workplace is doing.

Efficiency Estimation:

Key Execution Markers (KPIs):

Employee productivity can be quantitatively measured by establishing KPIs that are in line with the goals of the organization. Measurements like deals targets, project fulfillment times, and client fulfillment scores offer substantial bits of knowledge into execution levels.

Time and Undertaking Following:

Executing time-following instruments helps screen how representatives apportion their time all through the average business day. Examining the information can uncover designs, recognize bottlenecks, and advance work processes for expanded productivity.

Work Productivity:

The importance of evaluating the work's quality cannot be overstated. Ordinary assessments and criticism components can quantify the exactness, accuracy, and imagination exhibited in assignments. High-quality outputs frequently point to employees who are enthusiastic and engaged.

Use of Innovation:

Observing the utilization of innovation instruments and assets gives bits of knowledge into work process proficiency. Regular programming use and embracing innovation patterns might connote a labor force that adjusts well to developing workplaces.

Cooperation and Group Elements:

Solid group joint effort adds to generally efficiency. Noticing correspondence designs, project collaboration, and cross-useful participation can feature regions for development and measure the effect on efficiency.

Dynamic Interdependence:

Worker Commitment Overviews:

Consolidating parts of both spirit and efficiency, commitment overviews survey the general responsibility and association representatives feel toward their work and the association. Drawn in representatives are bound to be useful and contribute decidedly to the working environment air.

Health Projects:

Worker prosperity straightforwardly impacts both resolve and efficiency. Executing wellbeing programs further develops by and large work fulfillment as well as upgrades physical and emotional wellness, emphatically affecting efficiency.

Acknowledgment and Prizes:

Employee morale is boosted and high performance is encouraged by acknowledging and rewarding accomplishments. Perceiving commitments lines up with the association's objectives, building up a feeling of direction and worth.

All in all, estimating worker confidence and efficiency includes a diverse methodology that consolidates quantitative and subjective strategies. A positive work environment is created through regular accessments, feedback mechanisms, and a comprehensive comprehension of the dynamics of the organization. By consistently checking these pointers, organizations can adjust systems to improve both representative fulfillment and in general efficiency, eventually adding to long haul achievement.

Surveys and Feedback

Overviews and criticism systems assume an urgent part in different spaces, filling in as fundamental devices for organizations, associations, and people to accumulate significant data, survey execution, and pursue informed choices. These instruments have developed after some time, adjusting to mechanical progressions and changing correspondence scenes, while staying basic in grasping assessments, inclinations, and encounters.

Figuring out the Fundamentals

At its center, a review is a calculated way to deal with gathering information from an ideal interest group. Surveys aim to gather information on a wide range of topics, such as customer satisfaction, employee engagement, market trends, and more, whether they are carried out via traditional paper forms, over the phone, or online. The response or reaction to a specific experience, product, or service, on the other hand, is called feedback. Together, overviews and input systems make a powerful circle of data trade, empowering persistent improvement and refinement.

Significance in Business

In the business domain, overviews act as need might arise and inclinations. They give an immediate channel to organizations to accumulate criticism on their items or administrations, distinguish regions for development, and measure consumer loyalty. Client criticism is a compass that guides organizations in refining their contributions and fitting them to fulfill the developing needs of the market.

Additionally, representative studies are significant for measuring the spirit and commitment levels inside an association. By requesting criticism from representatives, organizations can recognize work environment challenges, upgrade correspondence, and establish a positive workplace. A fulfilled and drawn in labor force adds to expanded efficiency and cultivates a culture of development.

Innovative Progressions

The appearance of advanced innovations has altered the overview and criticism scene. Online reviews, email surveys, and intuitive web structures have made information assortment more proficient and open. The simplicity of overseeing computerized studies permits organizations to contact a more extensive crowd and gather constant input. Moreover, progressions in information examination empower associations to get significant experiences from huge datasets, working with information driven direction.

Web-based entertainment stages have additionally become instrumental in social affair criticism and figuring out open feelings. Organizations can use web-based entertainment channels to draw in with their crowd, address concerns, and gain significant bits of knowledge into market patterns. The prompt idea of online entertainment input empowers organizations to adjust rapidly to changing buyer assumptions.

Difficulties and Contemplations

While studies and criticism components offer various benefits, they are not without challenges. The phrasing of the questions, the length of the survey, and the demographics of the respondents all need to be carefully considered when designing effective surveys. The credibility of the insights gathered can be undermined by biased or unreliable data generated by poorly constructed surveys.

In addition, getting legitimate and valuable criticism can be a test, as respondents might be impacted by friendly attractiveness, predisposition or feeling of dread toward repercussions. Organizations should make a culture that energizes open correspondence and values input as a device for development instead of analysis.

The Development of Criticism

Past customary studies, criticism systems have been enhanced to incorporate different configurations like appraisals, surveys, and remarks. Online stages, particularly in the web based business and administration enterprises, depend vigorously on client surveys to construct trust and validity. User-generated content is transparent, giving potential customers genuine insights into the quality of products or services.

Continuous feedback from users assists developers in identifying bugs, improving features, and providing a more user-friendly experience. Feedback loops have also become an essential part of software development. Lithe systems, underscoring iterative turn of events and steady client input, influence criticism as a main thrust for development.

All in all, overviews and criticism components act as basic apparatuses for social event data, estimating fulfillment, and driving improvement across different areas. From forming business techniques to refining client encounters, the bits of knowledge got from reviews and input add to informed navigation. As innovation keeps on propelling, the advancement of these devices will probably carry much more refinement and accuracy to the specialty of understanding and answering the requirements and assumptions for people and markets the same.

Key Performance Indicators (KPIs)

Organizations use key performance indicators (KPIs) to evaluate and ovaluate their success in achieving particular business objectives. These markers act as navigational devices, directing chiefs in grasping the wellbeing and proficiency of different parts of their tasks. KPIs provide actionable insights that help businesses stay on course and adapt to changes in the business landscape, whether they are applied to financial performance, customer satisfaction, or internal processes.

In the domain of business, understanding and successfully using KPIs is much the same as having a dependable compass. These pointers go about as benchmarks against which associations can assess their headway, distinguish regions for development, and go with informed choices. It is essential to select relevant KPIs that are in line with the organization's strategic objectives and priorities. A focused and purpose-driven approach to performance measurement can be created with the help of a well-defined set of KPIs.

Monetary KPIs are among the most normally used pointers, mirroring the financial wellbeing and dependability of an association. Measurements like income development, overall revenues, and profit from venture give a thorough perspective on monetary presentation. By intently observing these markers, organizations can arrive at informed conclusions about asset allotment, venture techniques, and in general monetary administration.

Client driven KPIs are similarly fundamental, revealing insight into an association's capacity to meet client assumptions and keep up with fulfillment. Insights into the efficacy of marketing strategies, product quality, and the overall customer experience are provided by metrics like customer retention rates, Net Promoter Score (NPS), and customer lifetime value. By focusing on these KPIs, organizations can encourage long haul client connections and improve their upper hand.

Functional effectiveness is one more basic perspective tended to by KPIs. Associations frequently track measurements, for example, process duration, process effectiveness, and asset use to enhance inward cycles and work processes. These markers empower organizations to distinguish bottlenecks, smooth out tasks, and upgrade efficiency. By consistently observing functional KPIs, associations can adjust to changing economic situations and keep a deft and effective functional system.

Worker execution and fulfillment are fundamental parts of hierarchical achievement, and KPIs in this space assume a critical part. Measurements, for example, representative commitment, turnover rates, and efficiency per worker offer important experiences into the general well being of the labor force. Organizations that focus on these markers can execute designated methodologies to further develop worker spirit, cultivate a positive working environment culture, and at last improve general execution.

Key KPIs are intended to survey the outcome of an association in accomplishing its drawn out objectives and targets. These markers frequently include a mix of monetary, client, and functional measurements that line up with the essential course of the business. Organizations can assess their progress toward overarching goals and make necessary adjustments to their strategies by regularly evaluating strategic KPIs.

It's significant to perceive that the viability of KPIs depends intensely on exact information assortment and investigation. Executing hearty information the board frameworks and guaranteeing information trustworthiness are fundamental stages in the fruitful usage of KPIs. Also, KPIs ought to be dynamic and versatile, mirroring the developing idea of business conditions. Consistently rethinking and changing KPIs guarantees their significance and viability over the long haul.

While KPIs offer important bits of knowledge, it's fundamental for associations to stay away from the normal trap of over-burdening themselves with exorbitant measurements. Finding a balance between comprehensive measurement and practicality is crucial. Zeroing in on a reasonable arrangement of KPIs that straightforwardly line up with hierarchical objectives considers more successful checking and navigation.

organizations seeking to navigate the complex landscape of business success require the use of Key Performance Indicators. From monetary security to consumer loyalty, functional proficiency to worker execution, KPIs give a comprehensive perspective on hierarchical wellbeing. By choosing and checking these pointers prudently, organizations can keep on track, pursue informed choices, and consistently adjust to the powerful difficulties of the advanced business world.

Chapter 6
Creating a Festive Work Environment

Establishing a merry workplace is an incredible method for encouraging everyone, upgrading worker commitment, and cultivating a positive organizational culture. The Christmas season gives an ideal chance to infuse a little satisfaction and kinship into the work environment. There are a few ways to help create a festive atmosphere that will not only bring holiday cheer but will also make working there more fun and productive.

1. Enhance tho Work area:
Begin by enhancing the workplace with merry embellishments. Think about including traditional holiday decorations like wreaths, colorful ornaments, and twinkling lights. Be aware of various social festivals to guarantee inclusivity in your designs. Urge representatives to acquire individual embellishments to cause the work area to feel more customized and bubbly.

2. Set Up Theme Days:
During the holiday season, start dress-up days with themed themes. Whether it's a monstrous sweater day, occasion cap day, or even a pajama day, these carefree topics can bring a feeling of

tomfoolery and solidarity among workers. Ensure the topics are comprehensive and energize cooperation without causing distress.

3. Plan activities for team building:
Coordinate group building exercises that have a bubbly contort. Think about games with holiday themes, a secret Santa gift exchange, or even a decorating competition. These exercises can assist with reinforcing group securities, further develop correspondence, and make enduring recollections among partners.

4. Have a Merry Lunch or Potluck:
Gather everybody for a festive meal. Sharing a meal fosters a sense of community and celebration, whether it's a catered lunch, a potluck where employees bring their favorite holiday dishes, or a simple cookie exchange. Guarantee there are possibilities for different dietary inclinations and limitations.

5. Reward the Local area:
By organizing charitable events, you can spread holiday cheer outside of the office. This could be accomplished through a food drive, a toy drive, or team volunteering at a local charity. Offering back helps those deprived as well as ingrains a feeling of direction and generosity among workers.

6. Make an Occasion Playlist:
Set the state of mind with a bubbly playlist that incorporates occasion works of art and merry tunes. Permit workers to add to the playlist to guarantee an assorted choice that obliges different melodic preferences. Music has the ability to make an upbeat climate and lift

spirits all through the typical business day.

7. Energize Distant Festivals:

For remote or mixed groups, guarantee that the happy soul arrives at everybody. Arrange virtual festivals, like web based games, video gatherings, or virtual mystery St Nick trades. Giving open doors to far off representatives to take part in happy exercises cultivates a feeling of consideration and having a place.

8. Acknowledge Achievements:

Recognize and commend the achievements of the group consistently. This could incorporate a year-end grants function, customized notes of appreciation, or little badge of appreciation. A positive work environment is bolstered by recognizing individual and collective accomplishments.

9. Convey Assumptions Plainly:

While making a happy climate, it's fundamental to plainly impart any assumptions or ruloc. Make sure employees know how to strike a balance between celebrating and remaining professional. Help everybody to be careful to remember social responsive qualities and regard variety during the Christmas season.

10. Give Adaptable Timetables:

Recognize that for many employees, the holiday season can be a busy and stressful time. Offer adaptable plans for getting work done or extra downtime to oblige individual responsibilities and reduce pressure. This signal exhibits compassion and advances a sound balance between fun and serious activities.

decorations, activities, and a focus on team spirit are all needed to create a festive workplace. By consolidating these methodologies, you can implant the work environment with a feeling of delight and brotherhood during the Christmas season. Be inclusive, keep in mind individual preferences, and work to create an atmosphere where everyone can have a good time and be treated with respect.

Office Decorations and Inclusive Celebrations

Office embellishments assume an essential part in establishing a positive and comprehensive workplace. Past simple feel, insightful style can cultivate a feeling of local area, lift everyone's spirits, and improve the general work environment experience. With regards to festivities, inclusivity ought to be at the front, guaranteeing that all representatives feel regarded and esteemed. How about we investigate the meaning of office enrichments and procedures for comprehensive festivals.

Office Enrichments: Establishing a Positive Workplace

The actual work area is an impression of an organization's way of life and values. Decor that has been carefully thought of for the office helps create a warm and interesting atmosphere. Consider integrating components that reflect variety and inclusivity, like fine art, statements, or images from different societies. This sends a reasonable message that the work environment values and regards alternate points of view.

Besides, very much planned office spaces can emphatically influence representatives' psychological prosperity. A more pleasant and energizing atmosphere can be created by using plants, bright colors, and natural light. Customizing workstations with things that hold nostalgic worth or exhibit individual interests can cultivate a feeling of having a place.

In the majority of workplaces, teamwork and collaboration are essential. Style that empowers association, as public regions with open to seating or cooperative undertaking sheets, can upgrade the feeling of collaboration and brotherhood. Moreover, giving spaces to unwinding and calm reflection permits workers to re-energize, advancing by and large efficiency and occupation fulfillment.

Comprehensive Festivals: Esteeming Variety and Regard

Festivities are an indicpensable piece of working environment culture, giving open doors to representatives to interface and construct connections. Notwithstanding, it's urgent to guarantee that these festivals are comprehensive, embracing the variety of the labor force.

Different Festivals:

Commend various occasions and far-reaching developments consistently. This can be accomplished by showing enhancements that address various practices and customs. Recognize and regard the strict and social variety inside the group, guaranteeing that everybody feels remembered for the merriments.

All-inclusive Topics:

Choose themes that are inclusive and considerate of people from different backgrounds when planning office events. Stay away from topics that might avoid or make a few workers anxious. Instead, focus on themes that reflect the collective team's values, accomplishments, or milestones.

Correspondence and Responsiveness:

Allow employees to voice their preferences and concerns through open communication regarding celebrations, which should be prioritized. Be aware of how different people might react to celebrations. For instance, some might incline toward a calm festival, while others might appreciate more merry occasions. Conscious correspondence guarantees that everybody's inclinations are thought of.

Flexibility:

Perceive that not every person notices similar occasions or may have individual explanations behind not partaking in specific festivals. Offering adaptability in cooperation permits representatives to feel great while as yet being essential for the working environment of the local area.

Open Exercises:

Plan exercises that are open to all representatives, taking into account any physical or social restrictions. This guarantees that everybody can effectively take part in the festival without feeling rejected.

Contextual analysis: A Model Comprehensive Office Festivity

Envision an organization arranging a year-end festivity. Rather than zeroing in exclusively on a solitary occasion, the coordinators choose to embrace the variety of their group. They incorporate elements from a variety of cultures and traditions to create a theme called "Global Perspectives." The workplace is enhanced with designs addressing various nations, and the occasion includes a potluck where representatives can bring dishes that mirror their legacy.

All through the festival, there are open doors for workers to share tales about their social customs, cultivating understanding and appreciation among partners. Furthermore, the organization guarantees that the occasion is available to all representatives, giving choices to virtual cooperation for those unfit to go to face to face.

The company not only commemorates the year's accomplishments but also fosters a sense of unity and respect among its diverse workforce by adopting this inclusive strategy. This model can act as motivation for different associations hoping to make comprehensive and important office festivities.

All in all, office improvements and comprehensive festivals are vital parts of a positive work environment culture. Mindfully planned stylistic layout adds to an inviting climate, while comprehensive festivals reinforce the feeling of local area among representatives.

By embracing variety, regarding individual inclinations, and encouraging open correspondence, associations can make work areas that praise the extraordinary commitments of each and every colleague, at last prompting a more connected and agreeable work environment.

Chapter 7
Leadership Role in Balancing Work and Festivities

The delicate task of balancing work and celebrations necessitates effective leadership to ensure employee productivity and well-being. The holiday season brings both potential difficulties and excitement to any organization. A leader is essential in creating a work environment that celebrates and embraces the holiday spirit while remaining focused on the company's objectives.

One critical part of authority during the Christmas season is setting clear assumptions. Speaking with the group about work needs and cutoff times deals with everybody's time actually. Employees should be able to enjoy the festivities without having to compromise their professional responsibilities, so a leader should strike a balance. This clearness assists in forestalling with enduring moment surges and diminishes pressure among colleagues.

Adaptability is one more essential quality of a pioneer during this time. Recognizing that representatives might have individual responsibilities or occasion related liabilities exhibits sympathy. Offering adaptable work hours or remote work choices can be a significant method for obliging these requirements. Employee morale is raised and a positive work environment is maintained by this flexibility.

Besides, pioneers can effectively take part in making a happy environment inside the working environment. This can incorporate getting sorted out group building exercises, designing the workplace space, or arranging a special festival. Such drives encourage a feeling of brotherhood and lift group confidence level, adding to a more good workplace.

Nonetheless, it's pivotal for pioneers to be aware of social and strict variety inside their group. While praising merriments, it's fundamental to guarantee that exercises and enrichments are comprehensive and regard the assorted foundations of workers. This comprehensive methodology helps in making an amicable working environment where everybody feels esteemed and included.

As well as encouraging a merry air, pioneers ought to be mindful of the prosperity of their colleagues. The Christmas season can be distressing for certain people, whether because of individual reasons or expanded responsibilities. Pioneers can uphold their group by empowering breaks, giving assets to overseeing pressure, and being agreeable for any worries.

Correspondence is the key part of successful authority, particularly during the Christmas season. Customary registrations and group gatherings assist with keeping everybody in total agreement in regards to project progress and needs. Pioneers ought to be straightforward about assumptions and convey any progressions to timetables or work processes expeditiously. This open correspondence guarantees that everybody knows about the aggregate objectives and obligations.

Showing others how it's done is a useful asset in directing a group through the Christmas season. It sets a positive example for the team as a whole when leaders prioritize well-being and maintain a healthy work-life balance. Empowering representatives to get some much needed rest to re-energize and invest quality energy with friends and family builds up the significance of both expert and individual parts of life.

During the holiday season, it is essential to take a proactive approach to managing workloads. Pioneers can team up with their groups to design and focus on assignments, guaranteeing that significant cutoff times are met while permitting adaptability for special festivals. This cooperative methodology advances productivity as well as cultivates a feeling of shared liability and responsibility.

Perceiving and valuing the difficult work of representatives during the Christmas season is pivotal for keeping up with inspiration. Pioneers can offer thanks through customized messages, little motions, or in any event, sorting out an acknowledgment occasion. Recognizing and praising accomplishments, both of all shapes and sizes, adds to a positive work culture and supports a feeling of achievement.

At long last, pioneers ought to know about potential burnout among colleagues. The Christmas season, with its additional obligations and social assumptions, can overpower. Pioneers can relieve burnout by observing responsibilities, offering help where required, and empowering taking care of oneself practices. A group that feels upheld during testing times is bound to remain connected with and persuaded.

leadership is crucial in achieving a work-life balance within an organization. By setting clear assumptions, cultivating adaptability, making a happy air, and focusing on representative prosperity, pioneers can direct their groups through the Christmas season effectively. Compelling Initiative during this time adds to a positive workplace, reinforces group bonds, and guarantees that both work and merriments are given their due significance.

Leading by Example and Communication Strategies

Showing others how it's done is a basic rule in compelling authority that rises above enterprises and hierarchical designs. It includes exhibiting the qualities, hard working attitude, and conduct one anticipates from their colleagues. This initiative methodology is a useful asset for encouraging a positive and useful workplace.

A leader sets an example for their team when they lead by example. Whether it's reliability, responsibility, or a solid hard working attitude, the pioneer turns into a good example, moving others to copy their way of behaving. This approach makes a culture of responsibility and obligation inside the group, as individuals perceive the assumptions and endeavor to meet them.

Authenticity is one of the most important aspects of leading by example. Bona fide pioneers are authentic and straightforward, and they don't request that their group accomplish something they wouldn't do themselves. This forms trust and validity, fundamental parts of viable administration. At the point when colleagues see their chief trying to do they say others should do, they are bound to regard and heed their direction.

Correspondence is one more foundation of viable initiative. Clear, open, and genuine correspondence is significant for building solid connections inside a group. Pioneers should be proficient at passing on data, listening effectively, and giving input. Correspondence techniques that advance getting it and coordinated effort are fundamental for accomplishing shared objectives.

To show others how it's done in correspondence, pioneers ought to focus on undivided attention. This includes completely focusing on, understanding, and answering a speaker. By exhibiting undivided attention, pioneers show their colleagues that their perspectives and thoughts are esteemed. This cultivates a culture of open correspondence, where colleagues feel happy with offering their viewpoints and concerns.

Moreover, pioneers ought to be clear and compact in their own correspondence. Vagueness can prompt misconceptions and disarray. At the point when pioneers articulate their assumptions, objectives, and plans obviously, it assists colleagues with grasping their job and obligations, adding to a more productive and compelling work process.

Non-verbal correspondence is frequently underrated however it assumes a huge part in authority. Looks, non-verbal communication, and manner of speaking can convey more than words alone. Pioneers should know about their non-verbal signals to guarantee that they line up with their planned message. A positive and certain disposition can motivate trust in the group, while negative non-verbal prompts might make pressure or vulnerability.

Flexibility is one more urgent part of successful correspondence methodologies. Leaders should adapt their communication style to their team members' needs and preferences. A few people might favor composed correspondence, while others flourish in eye to eye corporations. Understanding these distinctions and adjusting specialized techniques appropriately upgrades the general viability of the pioneer.

Written communication skills are just as crucial as verbal communication skills. Pioneers frequently need to pass data on through messages, reports, or other composed records. Clear and succinct composing guarantees that the planned message is effectively figured out, lessening the gamble of distortion. A pioneer who can communicate thoughts articulately recorded as a hard copy adds to a more smoothed out and viable dynamic interaction.

Feedback is an effective instrument for personal and professional development. Pioneers ought to give useful input to assist their colleagues with further developing execution and accomplish their objectives. However, it is essential to provide feedback. Productive analysis ought to be conveyed in a positive and strong way, zeroing in on unambiguous ways of behaving as opposed to individual credits. This strategy inspires team members to strive for excellence and fosters a culture of continuous improvement.

To summarize, showing others how its done and viable correspondence systems are essential parts of fruitful administration. By encapsulating the qualities and ways of behaving they anticipate from their group, chiefs rouse trust and make a positive work culture. Clear, open, and versatile correspondence fabricates solid connections, cultivates coordinated effort, and adds to by and large group achievement. As pioneers embrace these standards, they not just aid their group towards accomplishing normal targets yet additionally develop a climate where people can flourish and arrive at their maximum capacity.

CONCLUSIO N

Strategies on Long-term Impact on Morale and Productivity

Creating compelling procedures for long haul influence on resolve and efficiency while adjusting work and celebrations is pivotal for cultivating a positive and practical workplace. As associations explore the difficulties of keeping up with worker prosperity and commitment, a comprehensive methodology that incorporates both expert and individual perspectives is fundamental.

Right off the bat, perceiving the meaning of representative assurance is basic. A persuaded labor force is in many cases a more useful one. Hence, carrying out methodologies that focus on worker prosperity can have an enduring positive effect. Ordinary registrations, open correspondence channels, and recognizing individual accomplishments add to a strong climate. Furthermore, giving open doors to proficient development and advancement can upgrade work fulfillment, lifting the general mood over the long haul.

Moreover, encouraging a positive work culture requires a harmony between keeping up with efficiency and recognizing the significance of celebrations. Associations ought to perceive and commend social and strict occasions, empowering variety and inclusivity. Making a schedule that obliges different festivals can help in arranging responsibilities and cutoff times, forestalling extreme pressure during merry periods.

Carrying out adaptable work courses of action is another key technique. A better work-life balance can be achieved by giving employees more control over their work hours or by offering remote work options. This adaptability adds to expanded confidence as well as improves efficiency as representatives can fit their timetables to more readily suit their singular necessities.

Likewise, advancing a feeling of local area inside the working environment is fundamental for long haul good effect. Group building exercises, both all through the workplace, can fortify connections among associates. These exercises add to a positive workplace as well as make an emotionally supportive network that encourages cooperation and efficiency.

Also, putting resources into worker health programs is critical for supporting spirit and efficiency. These projects can incorporate psychological wellness assets, wellness drives, and stress the board studios. By focusing on the prosperity of representatives, associations exhibit a guarantee to their labor force's drawn out well being and joy.

Effective time management is required to achieve work-life balance. Empowering representatives to prepare and set reasonable assumptions about responsibilities during occupied periods can forestall burnout. Giving direction on focusing on undertakings and designating liabilities can add to a smoother work process, guaranteeing that both work responsibilities and happy festivals are effectively obliged.

Finding some kind of harmony likewise includes powerful correspondence. Straightforward correspondence about assumptions during bubbly seasons, like any changed work hours or impermanent changes in project timetables, is urgent. This straightforwardness guarantees that everybody is in total agreement, decreasing likely misconceptions and stress.

Moreover, pioneers assume a significant part in establishing the vibe for a reasonable workplace. Showing others how its done, they ought to exhibit a pledge to balance between serious and fun activities and urge their groups to focus on both expert and individual prosperity. This initiative methodology cultivates a culture that values people past their jobs inside the association, adding to a positive and strong climate.

The techniques for long haul influence on confidence and efficiency while adjusting work and merriments are interconnected and require a thorough methodology. Focusing on representative prosperity, cultivating a positive work culture, carrying out adaptable work game plans, advancing local areas, putting resources into health programs, successfully using time effectively, and straightforward correspondence are essential parts.

By embracing and adjusting these systems, associations can develop a maintainable and flourishing working environment that meets proficient objectives as well as sustains the all encompassing prosperity of their labor force.

www.ingramcontent.com/pod-product-compliance
Lightning Source LLC
Chambersburg PA
CBHW062246290526
45794CB00006B/2434